AUDIO ACCESS INCLUDED
Recorded Piano Accompaniments Online

PLAYBACK+
Speed • Pitch • Balance • Loop

SINGER'S JAZZ ANTHOLOGY • LOW VOICE

standards

Arranged by Brent Edstrom

To access audio visit:
www.halleonard.com/mylibrary

"Enter Code"
3940-8747-2615-6531

ISBN 978-1-5400-4195-1

HAL•LEONARD®

Visit Hal Leonard Online at
www.halleonard.com

Contact us:
Hal Leonard
7777 West Bluemound Road
Milwaukee, WI 53213
Email: info@halleonard.com

In Europe, contact:
Hal Leonard Europe Limited
42 Wigmore Street
Marylebone, London, W1U 2RN
Email: info@halleonardeurope.com

In Australia, contact:
Hal Leonard Australia Pty. Ltd.
4 Lentara Court
Cheltenham, Victoria, 3192 Australia
Email: info@halleonard.com.au

ARRANGER'S NOTE

The vocalist's part in the *Singer's Jazz Anthology* matches the original sheet music but is *not* intended to be sung verbatim. Instead, melodic embellishments and alterations of rhythm and phrasing should be incorporated to both personalize a performance and conform to the accompaniments. In some cases, the form has been expanded to include "tags" and other endings not found in the original sheet music. In these instances, the term *ad lib.* indicates new melodic material appended to the original form.

Although the concept of personalizing rhythms and embellishing melodies might seem awkward to singers who specialize in classical music, there is a long tradition of melodic variation within the context of performance dating back to the Baroque. Not only do jazz singers personalize a given melody to fit the style of an accompaniment, they also develop a distinctive sound that helps *further* personalize their performances. Undoubtedly, the best strategy for learning how to stylize a jazz melody is to listen to recordings from the vocal jazz canon, including artists such as Nat King Cole, Ella Fitzgerald, Billie Holiday, Frank Sinatra, Sarah Vaughan, Nancy Wilson, and others.

The accompaniments in the *Singer's Jazz Anthology* can also be embellished by personalizing rhythms or dynamics, and chord labels are provided for pianists who are comfortable playing their own chord voicings. In some cases, optional, written-out improvisations are provided. These can be performed "as is," embellished, or skipped, depending on the performers' preference.

The included audio features piano recordings that can be used as a rehearsal aid or to accompany a performance. Tempi were selected to fit the character of each accompaniment, and the optional piano solos were omitted to provide a more seamless singing experience for vocalists who utilize them as backing tracks.

I hope you find many hours of enjoyment exploring the *Singer's Jazz Anthology* series!

Brent Edstrom

BLUE SUEDE SHOES

Words and Music by
CARL LEE PERKINS

ALFIE
Theme from the Paramount Picture ALFIE

Words by HAL DAVID
Music by BURT BACHARACH

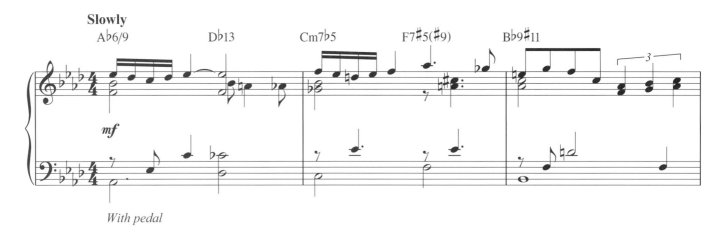

Slowly

What's it all a-bout, Al - fie? _____ Is it

just for the mo-ment we live? What's it all a-bout _____ when you sort it out, _

BAND OF GOLD

Words and Music by EDYTHE WAYNE
and RONALD DUNBAR

THE BEST IS YET TO COME

Music by CY COLEMAN
Lyrics by CAROLYN LEIGH

19

BLACKBIRD

Words and Music by JOHN LENNON
and PAUL McCARTNEY

Slowly and smoothly

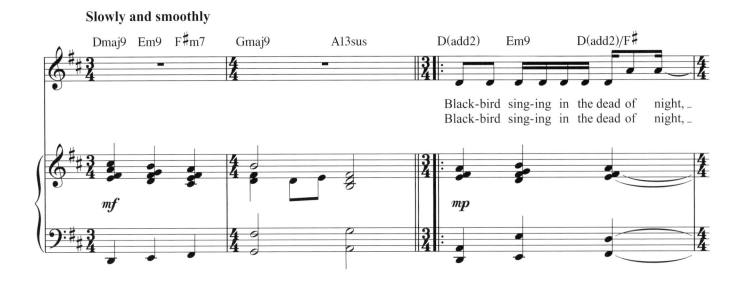

Black-bird sing-ing in the dead of night, _
Black-bird sing-ing in the dead of night, _

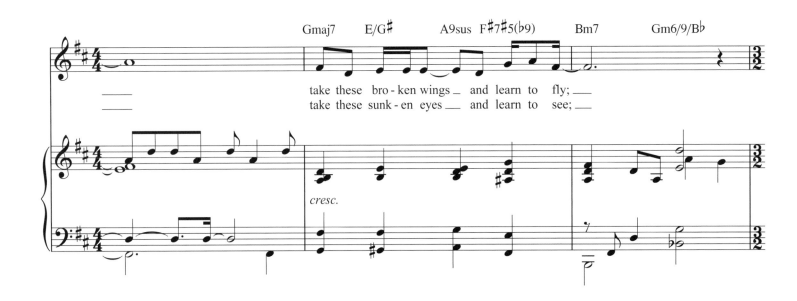

take these bro-ken wings _ and learn to fly; _
take these sunk-en eyes _ and learn to see; _

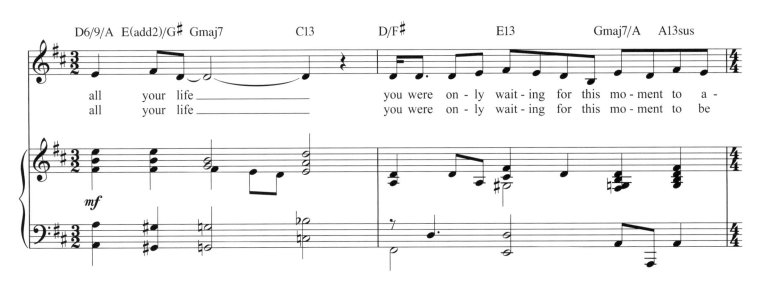

all your life ____ you were on-ly wait-ing for this mo-ment to a-
all your life ____ you were on-ly wait-ing for this mo-ment to be

22

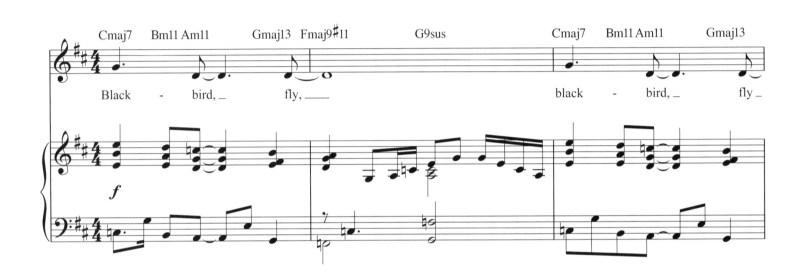

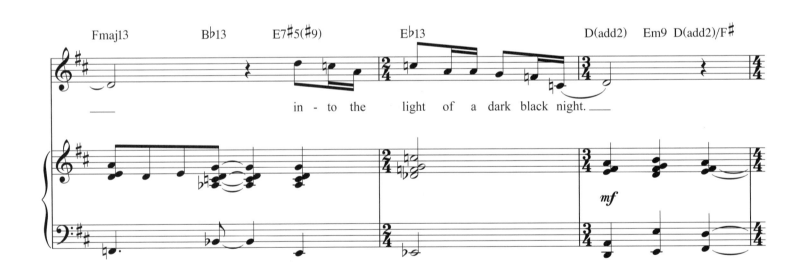

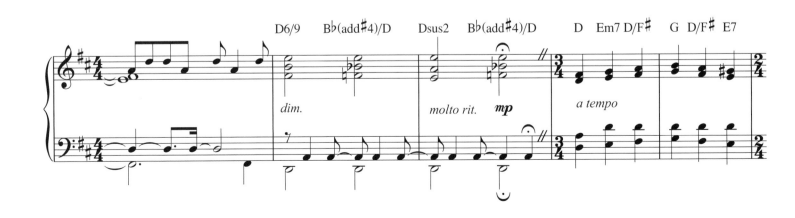

BRIDGE OVER TROUBLED WATER

Words and Music by
PAUL SIMON

I will lay me down.

Sail on, sil - ver girl, sail on

DREAM A LITTLE DREAM OF ME

Words by GUS KAHN
Music by WILBUR SCHWANDT and FABIAN ANDREE

EVERY BREATH YOU TAKE

Music and Lyrics by
STING

Ev - 'ry breath you take,

ev - 'ry move you make,

ev - 'ry bond you break,

I keep cry - ing, ba - by, ba - by, please. ___

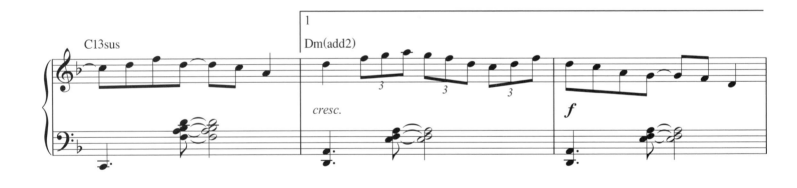

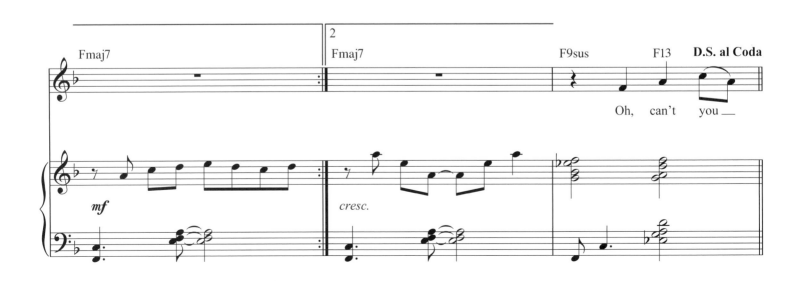

Oh, can't you ___

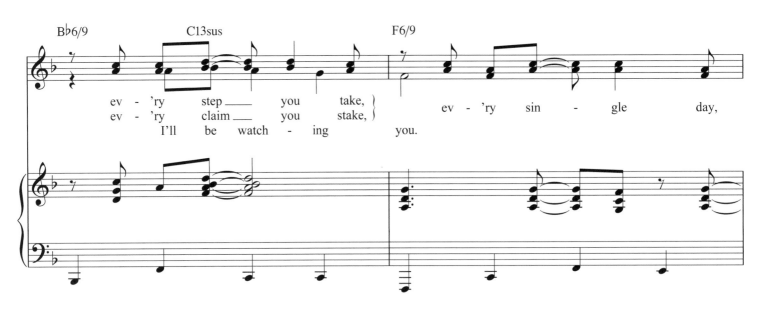

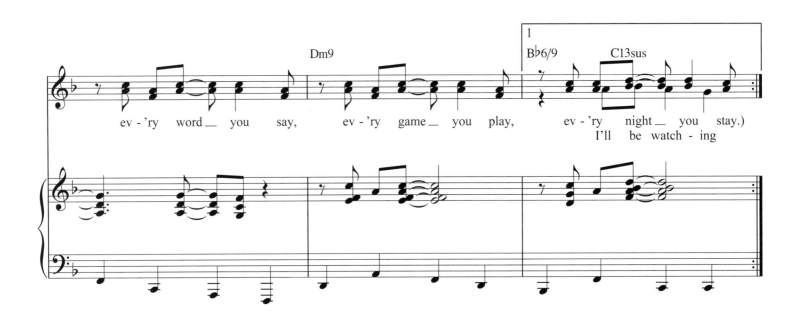

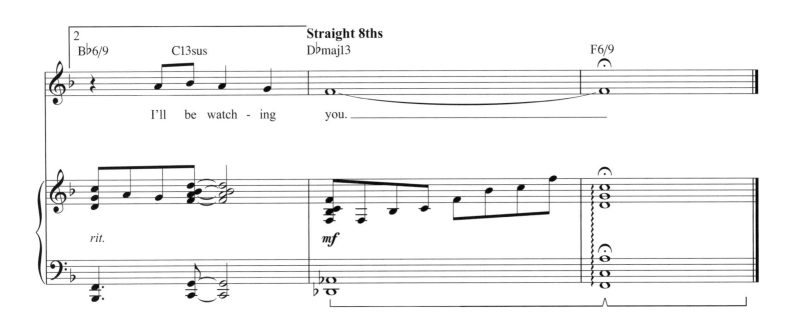

THE LOOK OF LOVE
from CASINO ROYALE

Words and Music by HAL DAVID
and BURT BACHARACH

FIRE AND RAIN

Words and Music by
JAMES TAYLOR

Slow Latin groove

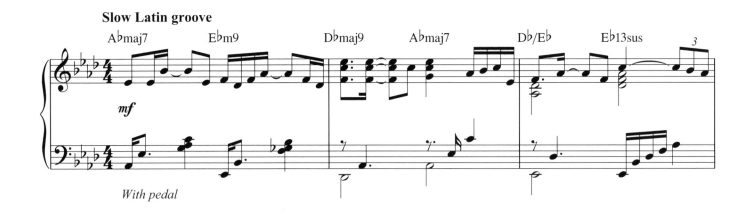

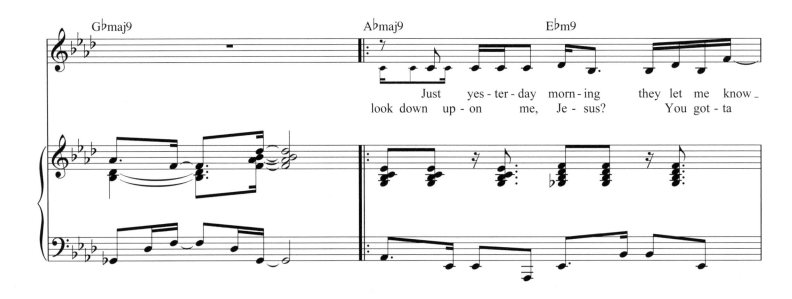

Just yes-ter-day morn-ing they let me know
look down up-on me, Je-sus? You got-ta

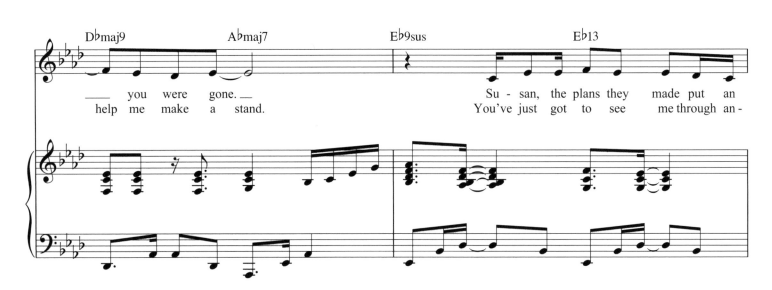

___ you were gone. ___
help me make a stand.

Su-san, the plans they made put an
You've just got to see me through an-

GOODBYE YELLOW BRICK ROAD

Words and Music by ELTON JOHN
and BERNIE TAUPIN

Moderately slow Swing

When are you gon - na come down?
What do you think you'll do then? I

When are you going to land? __
bet that'll shoot down your plane. __
I should have stayed __ on the farm.
It - 'll take you a cou - ple of vod -

I should have lis - tened to my __ old man. __
- ka and ton - ics to set you on your feet a - gain. __
You

50

I CAN'T STOP LOVING YOU

Words and Music by
DON GIBSON

Those   hap - py

you. ____

I HEARD IT THROUGH THE GRAPEVINE

Words and Music by NORMAN J. WHITFIELD
and BARRETT STRONG

ISN'T SHE LOVELY

Words and Music by
STEVIE WONDER

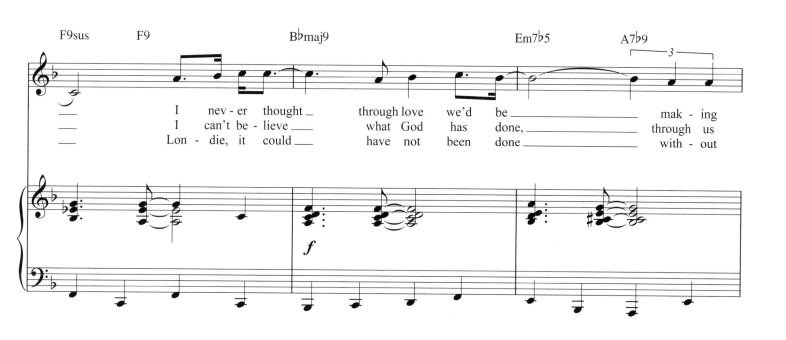

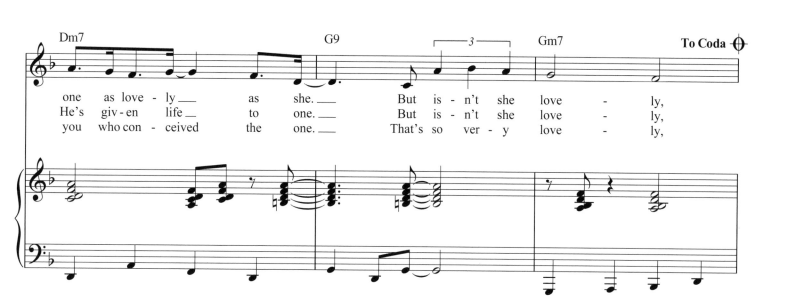

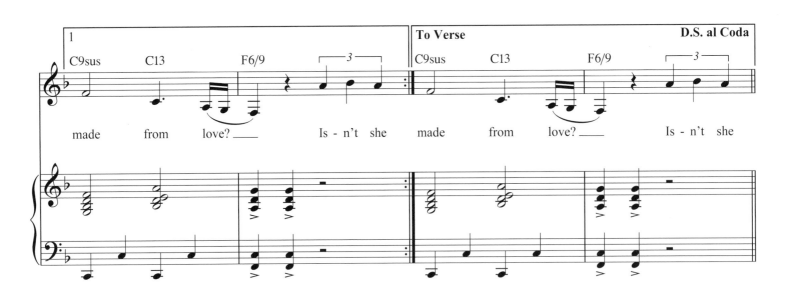

To Verse   **D.S. al Coda**

made   from   love? _____   Is - n't she   made   from   love? _____   Is - n't she

To Opt. Piano Solo

made   from   love. _____

MEDITATION
(Meditação)

Music by ANTONIO CARLOS JOBIM
Original Words by NEWTON MENDONÇA
English Words by NORMAN GIMBEL

ROLLING IN THE DEEP

Words and Music by ADELE ADKINS
and PAUL EPWORTH

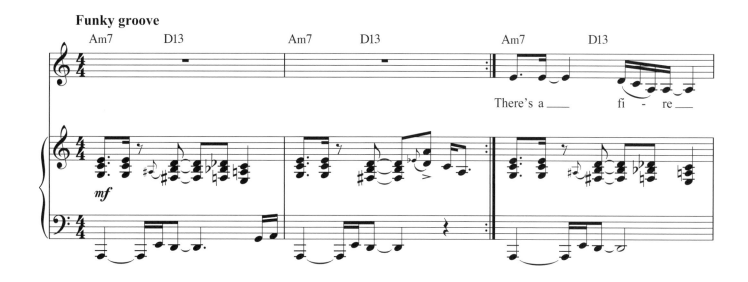

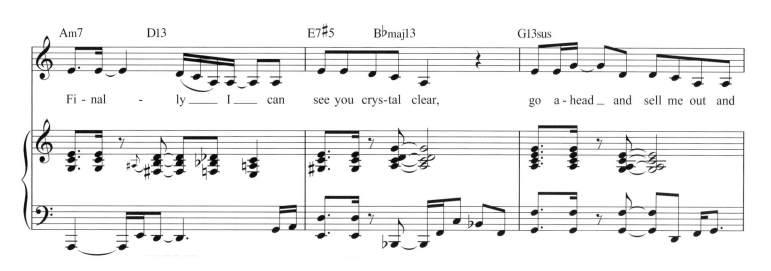

SINCERELY

Words and Music by ALAN FREED
and HARVEY FUQUA

(Sittin' On)
THE DOCK OF THE BAY

Words and Music by STEVE CROPPER
and OTIS REDDING

UNCHAIN MY HEART

Words and Music by BOBBY SHARP
and TEDDY POWELL

D♭9

Fm(add2)   B♭m6   Fm(add2)

B♭m6   Fm(add2)   D♭13   C7♯9

Fm   N.C.   **D.S. al Coda (take 2nd ending)**   **CODA**   Fm6   B♭m6

Un - chain my heart. __

(Vocal ad lib. on repeats)

dim.

Play 4 times

Fm6   Fm(add2)   B♭9

Oh, won't you set   me   free? _____

f

8vb

SWEET DREAMS
(Are Made of This)

Words and Music by ANNIE LENNOX
and DAVID STEWART

Some of them want to use ____ you. Some of them want to get used ____

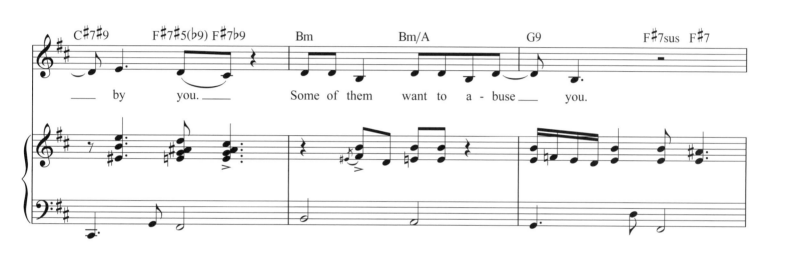

____ by you. ____ Some of them want to a - buse ____ you.

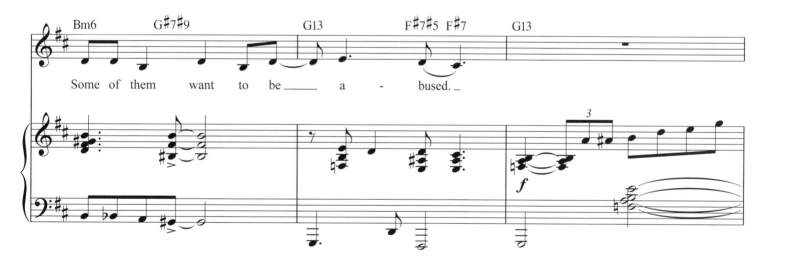

Some of them want to be ____ a - bused. ____

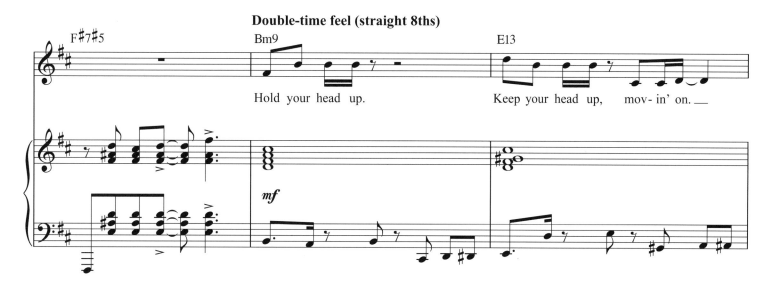

Double-time feel (straight 8ths)

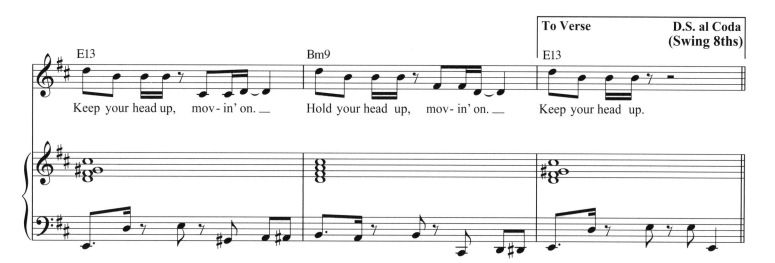

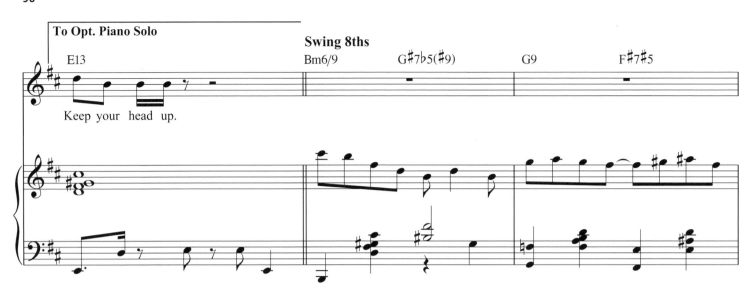

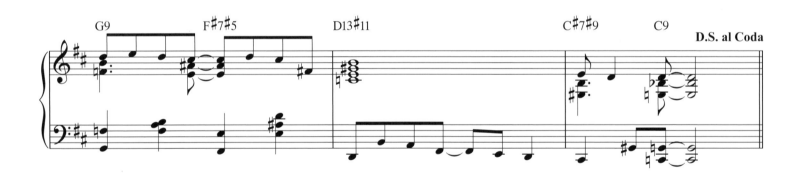

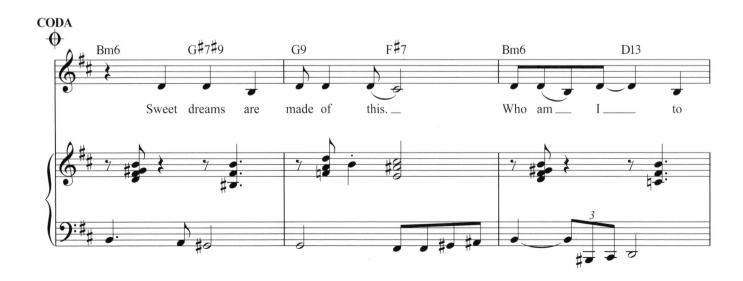

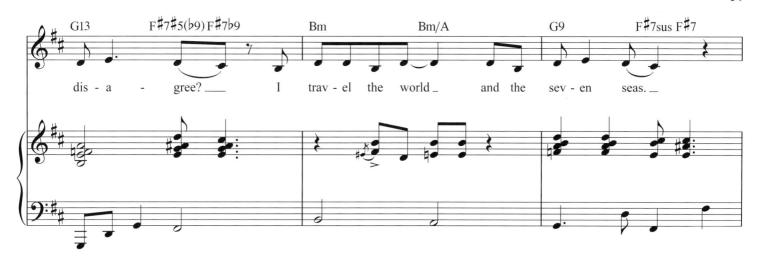

dis - a - gree? ___ I trav-el the world _ and the sev-en seas. _

Ev - 'ry-bod - y's look-ing for some - thing.

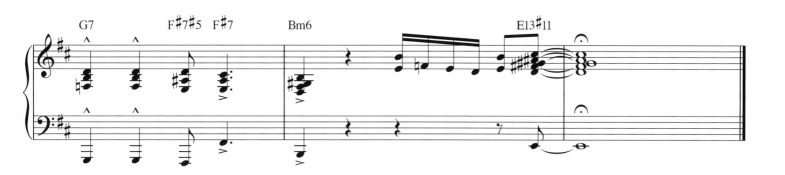

THREE TIMES A LADY

Words and Music by
LIONEL RICHIE

Jazz Waltz

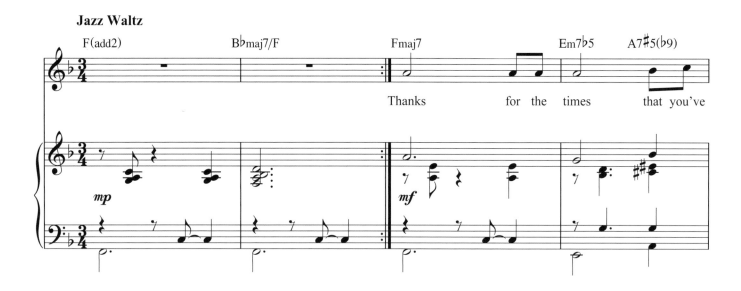

Thanks for the times that you've

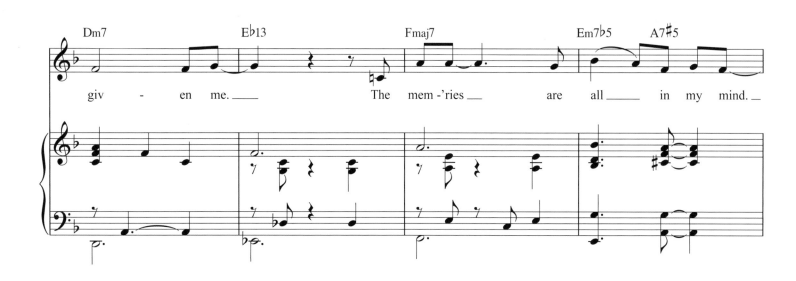

giv - en me. The mem -'ries are all in my mind.

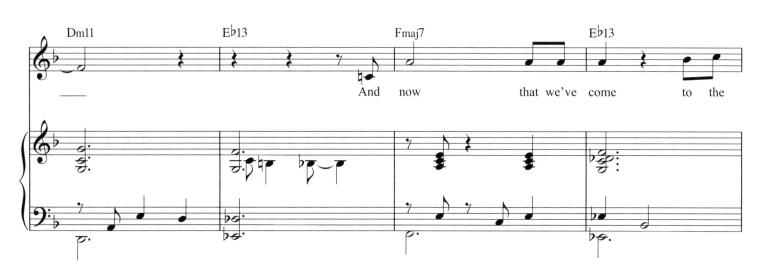

And now that we've come to the

WHAT THE WORLD NEEDS NOW IS LOVE

Lyric by HAL DAVID
Music by BURT BACHARACH

With a Jazz Waltz feel

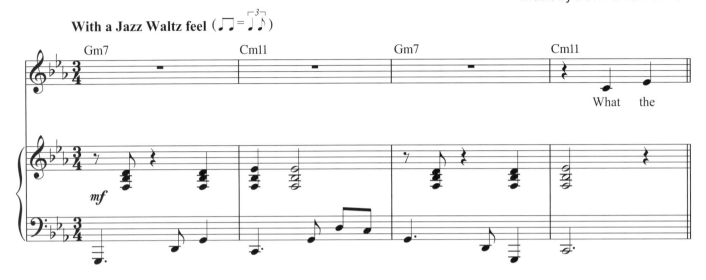

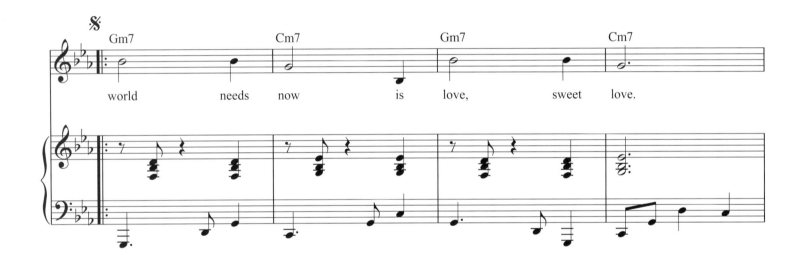

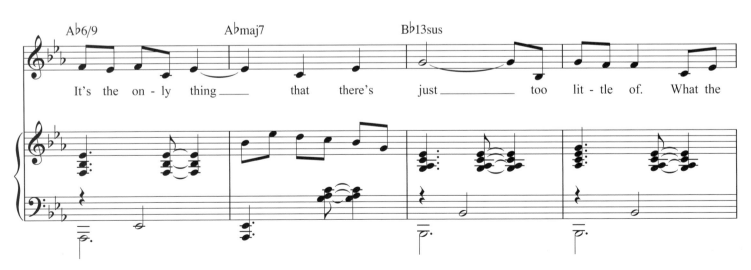

WITCHCRAFT

Music by CY COLEMAN
Lyrics by CAROLYN LEIGH

YESTERDAY

Words and Music by JOHN LENNON
and PAUL McCARTNEY

Jazz Ballad

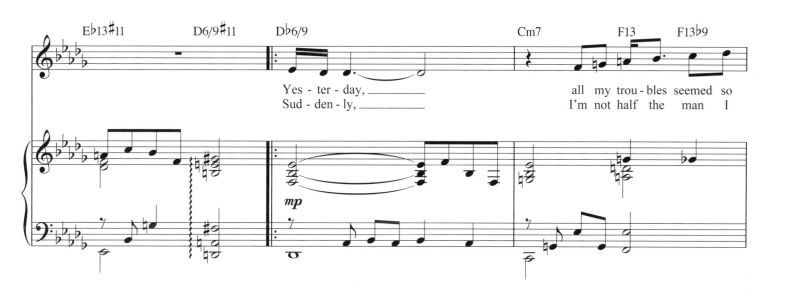

Yes - ter - day, _____ all my trou - bles seemed so
Sud - den - ly, _____ I'm not half the man I

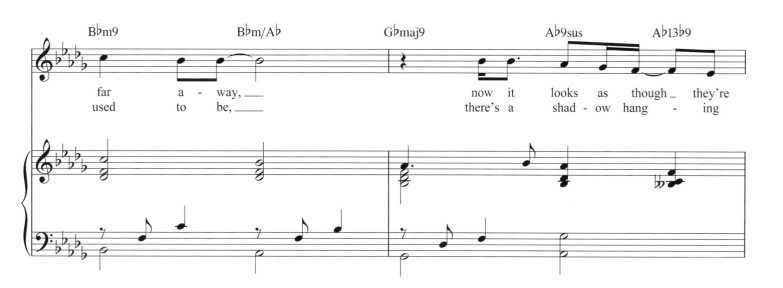

far a - way, _____ now it looks as though _ they're
used to be, _____ there's a shad - ow hang - ing

108

YOU ARE THE SUNSHINE OF MY LIFE

Words and Music by
STEVIE WONDER